Simplified Powerful FOREX Strategy

Isaackings

TABLE OF CONTENTS

CHAPTER 1: INTRODUCTION

CHAPTER 2: WHAT IS PRICE ACTION?

CHAPTER 3: UNDERSTANDING PRICE ACTION (mass trading psychology)

CHAPTER 4: INDENTIFYING REVERSALS AND CONTINUATION POINTS

CHAPTER 5: UNDERSTANDING MARKET SWINGS

CHAPTER 6: HOW TO TRADE SUPPPRT AND RESISTANCE

CHAPTER 7: HOW TO TRADE CHANNELS

CHAPTER 8: SEVEN (7) PROFITABLE CHART PATTERNS EVERY TRADER NEEDS TO KNOW

CHAPTER 9: SIX (6) PROFITABLE CANDLESTICKS PATTEEN EVERY TRADER NEEDS TO KNOW

CHAPTER 10: HOW TO TRADE TRENDLINES WITH PRICE ACTION

CHAPTER 11: MULTI-TIMEFRAME ANALYSIS

CHAPTER 12: TRADE THE OBVIOUS

CHAPTER 13: SECRET MARKET TIPS

CHAPTER 15: CLOSING REMARK .

CHAPTER 1:
INTRODUCTION

This powerful forex strategy is based on Pure Price Action(PPC)
Pure price action is simply a system of trading that uses Naked chart(chart without any indicators) to analyze and trade the forex markets,
this is the secret through which all other forex strategies is built
because major price determinant in any market are the BUYERS AND SELLERS ,

Before you get started, these are some words that you may encounter:
Long= buy
Short= sell
Bulls= buyers
Bears= sellers
Bullish=if the market is up, it is said to be bullish (uptrend).
Bearish=if the market is down, it's said to be bearish.
Bearish Candlestick=a candlestick that has opened higher and closed lower is said
to be bearish.
Bullish Candlestick=a candlestick that has opened lower and closed higher is said
to be a bullish candlestick.
Risk : Reward Ratio=if you risk $50 in a trade to make $150 then your risk: reward
is 1:3 which simply means you made 3 times more than your risked. This is an
example of risk: reward ratio.

CHAPTER 2:.
WHAT IS PRICE ACTION?

Price action is simply the effect of buyers and sellers actions on price. You can also define it as the effect of demand and supply on price.

ADVANTAGES OF PRICE ACTION TRADING

3 Important Reasons Why You Should Be Trading Price Action

1. **Price action represents collective human behavior.**

Human behavior in the market creates some specific patterns on the charts. So price action trading is really about understanding the psychology of the market using those patterns. That's why you see price hits support levels and bounces back up. That's why you see price hits resistance levels and heads down. Why? Because of collective human reaction!

2. Price action gives structure to the forex market.

You can't predict with 100% accuracy where the market will go next. However with price action, you can, to an extent predict where the market can potentially go. This is because price action brings structure. So if you know the structure, you can reduce the uncertainty to some extent and predict with some degree of certainty where the market will go next.

3. Price Action helps reduce noise and false signals.

If you are trading with stochastic or CCI indicators etc, they tend to give too false signals. This is also the case with many other indicators. Price action helps to reduce these kinds of false signals. Price action is not immune to false signals but it is a much better option than using other indicators…which are essentially derived from the raw price data anyway. Price action also helps to reduce "noise". What is noise? Market noise is simply all the price data that distorts the picture of the underlying trend… this is mostly due to small price corrections as well as volatility. One of the best ways to minimize market noise is to trade from larger timeframes instead of trading from smaller timeframes. See the 2 charts below to see what I mean.

TYPES OF PRICE ACTION

There are 2 types of price action trading,

The 100% Pure price action trading and the not-so-pure price Action trading. Let me explain…

Pure Price Action Trading

Pure price action trading simply means 100% price action trading. No indicators except price action alone as I said earlier in the introduction of this book.

Not-So-Pure Price Action Trading

This is when price action trading is used with other indicators and these other indicators form part of the price action trading system. These indicators can be trend indicators like moving averages or oscillators like stochastic indicator and CCI. (Please don't go googling CCI and stochastic indicators!)

Origin of Price Action Trading

Charles Dow is the guy credited to be the father of technical analysis. He came up with the DOW Theory.

The theory tries to explain market behavior and focuses on market trends. One part of the theory is that the market price discounts everything. Therefore, technical analysts use price charts and chart patterns to study market and don't really care about the fundament aspects of what move the markets.

The Dow Theory Of Trends Summarized

The theory in simple terms says that:

1. when price is in an uptrend, prices will be making increasing higher highs and higher lows until a higher low gets intercepted, then that signals the end of the uptrend and the beginning of a downtrend.

2. For downtrend, prices will be making increasing lower highs and lower lows until a lower low is intercepted and that signals an end of the downtrend and a beginning of an uptrend.

Structure of An Uptrend (Bull) Market

With an uptrend market, prices will be making higher highs (HH) and Higher Lows (HL)

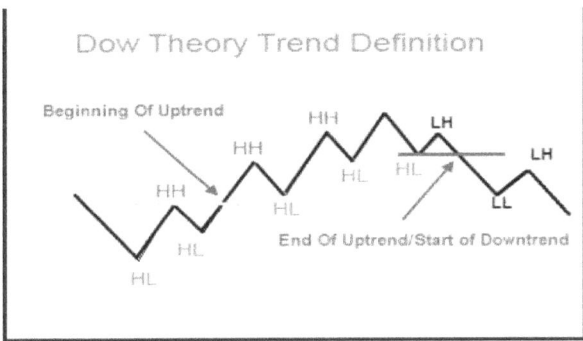

The reverse is the case for downtrend.

But you know that in reality, the market is not like this image above, it's more like this chart shown below:

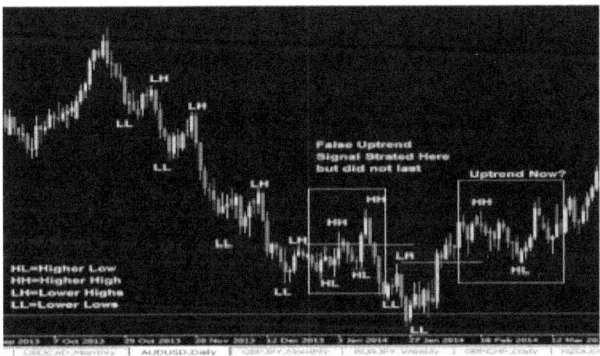

The chart above shows an initial downtrend and along the way there is a false uptrend which does not last and price moves down and then eventually another uptrend moves is happening because another lower high has been intersected(which signals end of downtrend).

This is how you use price action to identify trends. You should know this stuff.

Because the market is not perfect when these trends are happening, you should develop the skill to judge when a trend is still intact or when a trend is potentially reversing. And it's pretty much price intersecting highs or lows.

CHAPTER 3:.

UNDERSTANDING PRICE ACTION (mass trading psychology)

Here's one thing about price action: it represents a collective human behavior or mass psychology.

Let me explain.

All human beings have evolved to respond to certain situations in certain ways. And you can see this happen in the trading world as well:

The way multitude of traders think and react form patterns... repetitive price patterns that one can see and then predict with a certain degree of accuracy where the market will most likely go once that particular pattern is formed.

For example, if you see a major resistance level, price hits the level and forms a 'shooting star' a bearish reversal candlestick pattern. You can then say with a greater degree of confidence that Price is going to head down.

Why?

Because there are so many trader watching that resistance level and they all know that price has been rejected from this level on a previous one or two occasions and that tells them that it is a resistance level and that they can also see that bearish reversal candlestick formation… and guess what they will be waiting to do?

1. They will be waiting with their sell orders…not just one sell order but thousands of them, some small and some big orders.

2. But on the other side of the coin is that trader that have bought at a low price and now that the price is heading up to the resistance level, that's where most of their take profit levels are. So once they take their profits around resistance levels, that means there are now less buyers now and more sellers. The balance tips in the direction of the sellers and that's how the price is pushed back down from a resistance level.

Because price action is a representation of mass psychology…the markets are moved by the activities of traders.

So price action trading is about understanding the psychology of the market using those patterns and making a profit as a result.

CHAPTER 4:.

INDENTIFYING REVERSAL & CONTINUATION POINTS

A reversal is a term used to describe when a trend reverses direction. For example, the market has been in an uptrend and when price hits a major resistance level, it reversed and formed a downtrend. That's what reversal means.

Now where can reversals happen?

The following are the major areas where price reversals do happen:

- **Support levels**
- **Resistance levels**

Support level is simply a level on your chart where price reached and then reversed back upwards.

Resistance level is a region or level on your chart where price reached and then reversed back downwards.

Note:. When price fully breaks a support level ,the support level becomes a resistance level, and also when fully price breaks a resistance level, the resistance now becomes a support level.

So the big question is: how to spot trend continuity/reversal and execute trades at the right time?

The secret is in identification of specific chart patterns as well as very specific
candlesticks patterns and you will discover more on the Chart Patterns and
Candlestick Patterns section of this course.

Top 3 reasons why it is so important for you knowing reversal points/levels as well as understanding trend continuity patterns and signals:

1. You don't want to be buying near or at a resistance level (which is a reversal point).

2. You don't want to be selling at near or at a support level (which is a reversal point).

3. You don't want be buying when the trend is down and you don't want to be selling when the trend is up that's why you need to know about continuation charts and candlestick patterns which will allow you to trade with the trend.

(There are exceptions though when you can trade against the main trend like that like in trading channels...see Chapter 7 : How To Trade Channels)

CHAPTER 5:.
UNDERSTANDING MARKET SWINGS

Market Price moves in swings. A price swing is when markets moves like what a wave does.

So in an uptrend, price will be making higher highs and higher lows.

So in an uptrend, price moves in swings like this chart shown below:

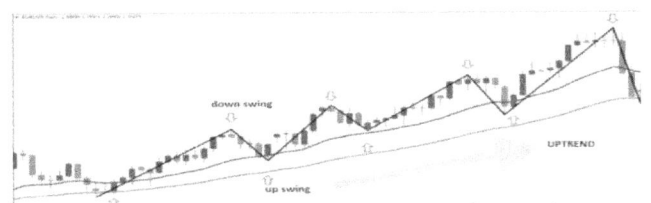

The reverse of this is for downtrend .

Those who opens trades at the beginning of a swing and sets Take profit or closes at the next swing are called swing traders .

Why it's So Important For You To Understand Market Price Swing

If you want to be really good price action trader, you have to understand this concept of how price moves in swings. This is especially true if since this strategy encompasses trend and swing trading which you're going to be using in your trading.

Because if you don't understand how price moves in swings, this is what you are going to end up doing:
1. You will execute trades at the very wrong spot! For example, in a downtrend, you will sell when the market is just doing an upswing! Not good!

2. Which means, you will get stopped out or you need to put in a large stop loss. Large stop loss does not necessarily mean large risk if you do position sizing based on the stop loss distance. But if you don't then that's a large risk you are taking.

3. If you have a large stop loss, then you've got to wait a while before the market makes downswing before you to start seeing profits on your trade.
Here's an example of what I'm talking about:

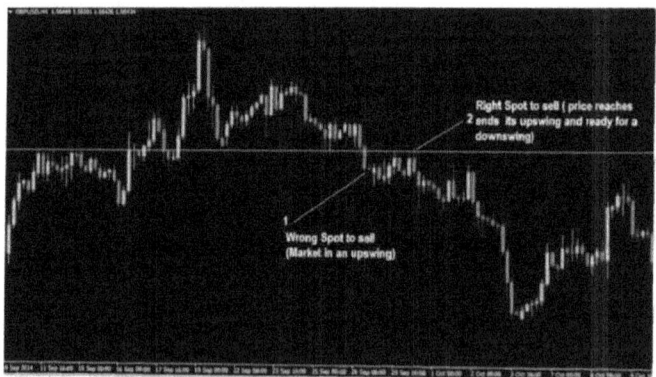

It's really not a good situation to be in. Every traders wish is that "the moment a trade is placed, it goes to profit immediately." But we know the market is not like
that, sometimes that happens, and sometimes it doesn't. That's the nature of the market.

So in an uptrend, you should be looking to buy on the downswing. In a downtrend, you should be looking to sell on an upswing.

And the best way for doing that is by using Price Action (reversal candlesticks):

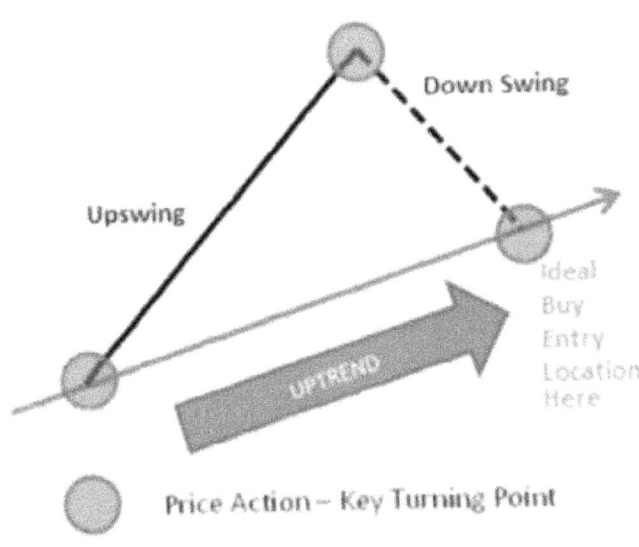

Real chart example:.

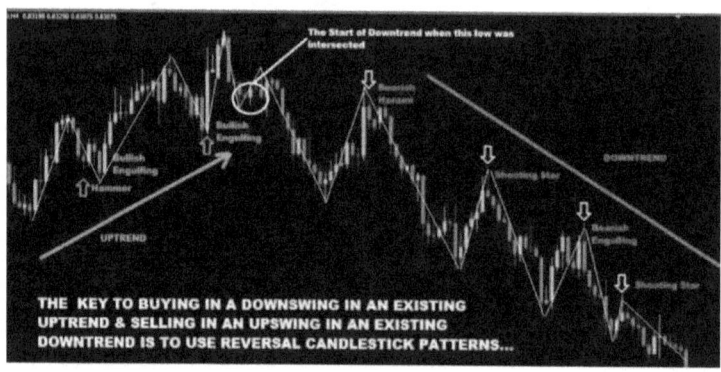

CHAPTER 6:.
HOW TO TRADE SUPPORT AND RESISTANCE LEVELS

Nothing is more noticeable on any chart than support and resistance levels. These levels stand out and are so easy for everyone to see! Why? Because they are so obvious.

As a matter of fact, support and resistance trading is the core of price action trading.
The key to successful price action trading lies in
finding effective support and resistance levels on your charts.

Now, in here, I talk about 3 types of support and resistance levels and they are:

1. The normal horizontal support and resistance levels that you are probably most familiar about.
2. Broken support levels become resistance levels and broken resistance levels become support levels.
3. Dynamic Support and Resistance Levels

Now, let's look at each in much more detail.

Horizontal Support and Resistance Levels

These are fairly easy to spot on your charts. They look like peaks and troughs.
The chart below is an example and shows you to trade them.

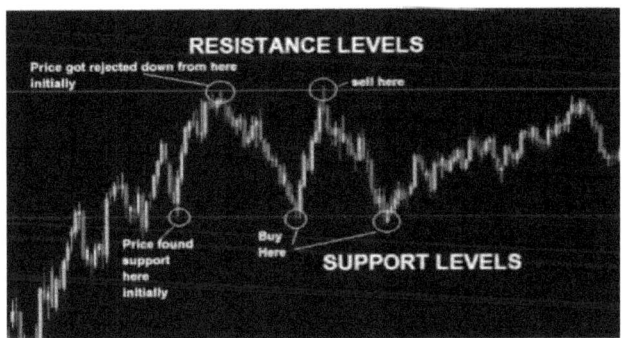

How To Find Horizontal Support And Resistance Levels On Your Chart

- If price has been going down for some time and hits a price level and bounces up from there, that's called a support level.
- Price goes up, hits a price level or zone where it cannot continue upward any further and then reverses, that's a resistance level.

So when price heads back to that support or resistance level, you should expect that it will get rejected from that level again.

The use of reversal candlestick
trading on support and resistance levels becomes very handy in these cases.

Significant Support & Resistance Levels
Not all support and resistance levels are created equal. If you really want to take trades that have high potential for success, you should focus on identifying significant support and resistance levels on your charts.

Significant support and resistance levels are those levels that are formed in the *large timeframes* like the monthly, weekly and daily charts.

And when price reacts to these levels, they usually tend to move for a very long time.

Now, here's the technique I use to trade setups that happen in larger timeframes:

I switch to smaller timeframes like the 4hr & the 1hr, 30min, 15min and even the 5min and wait for a reversal candlestick signal for my trade entries. This is so that I can get in at a much better price level as well as reducing my stop loss distance. But me personally I use 4hr majorly to find entries, and sometimes 1hr for confirmation.

That's what's multi-timeframe trading is all about. Support turned Resistance Level And Resistance Turned Support Level

Now, the next on is this thing called Support turned Resistance Level And Resistance Turned Support Level.

There are many traders that don't realize that usually, in a downtrend, when a support level has been broken to the downside, it often tends to act as a resistance level. Here is an example shown on the chart below:

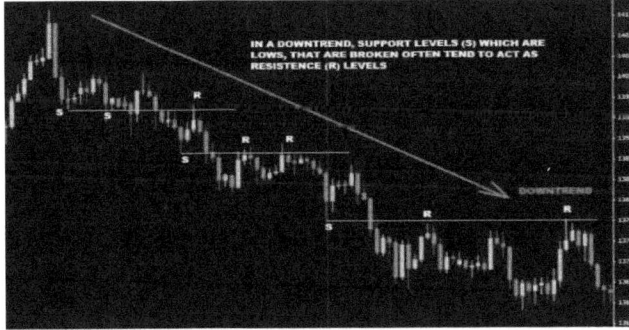

So when you see such happening, you should be looking for bearish reversal candlestick to go short. As a matter of fact these "R's" are the upswings in a downtrend.

Similarly, in an uptrend you will also see such happening where Resistance levels get broken and when price heads back down to these, they now will act as support levels...

Here's an example:

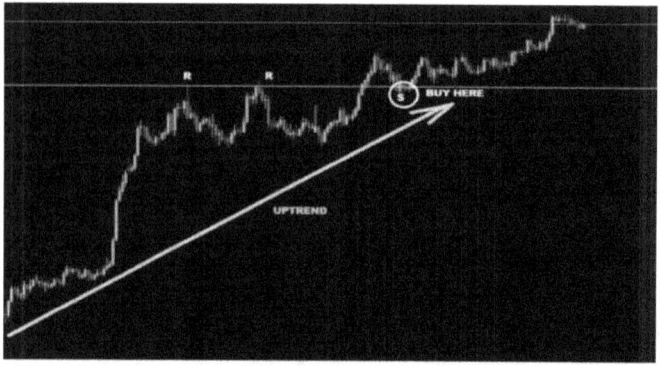

Look for bullish reversal candlestick around these type of resistance turned support levels as your signal to buy.

Can you see how the need for using other indicators is diminished once you understand how easy is to spot such trading setups like these?

CHAPTER 7 :.

HOW TO TRADE CHANNELS

What is a channel? And How Do You Trade A Channel? This section is about that.

The path price follows and the area enclosed within it is called the price channel.

The fundamental principle of how a channel form is based on support and resistance. Why price does that, I don't know… but consider it as supply and demand at work.

There are 3 major types of channels:

1. the uptrend channel,

2. the downtrend channel and

3. the sideways/horizontal channel.

This image below is what a downtrend channel looks like and how to trade it:

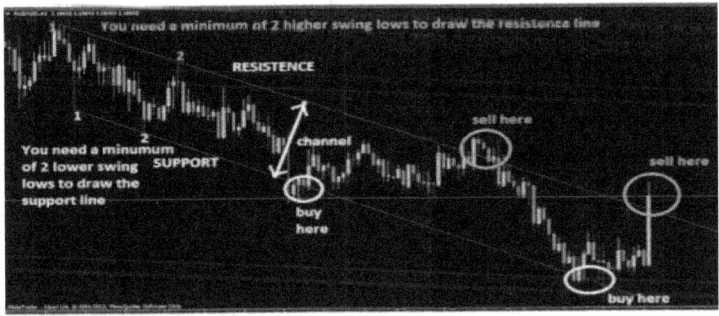

This image below is what an uptrend channel looks like and shows how you can trade it:

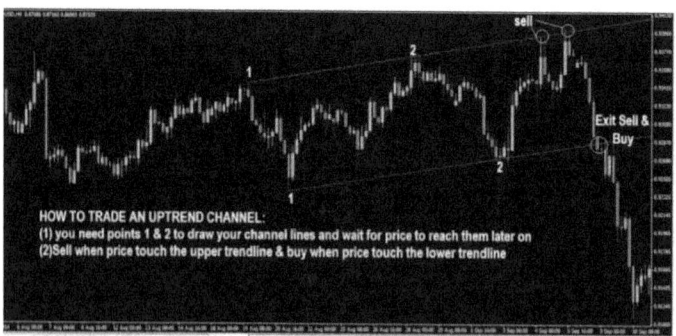

This chart below is what a sideways channel looks like and how you can trade it:

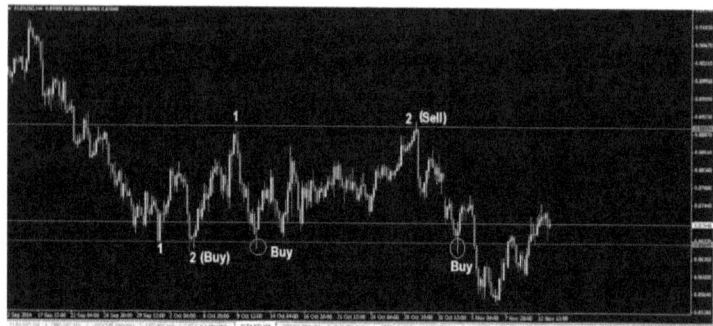

Sideways channels (or horizontal channels) are little bit different from uptrend and downtrend channels because with uptrend and downtrend channels, you
would require 2 points to draw trend lines and wait for price to touch them later on before you take a trade because the trend lines are at an angle.

But with sideways/horizontal channels, you can actually start trading the setup at point #2 which can be both a resistance or support level based on the fact that a prior resistance or support level is already visible and you should expect price to bounce from those levels.
Look for reversal candlesticks to buy or sell when you
see such setups happening.

Here Are Some General Rules For Trading Channels
1. If you buy or sell on the other side of the channel, you wait for price to reach the other end of the channel to take profit or exit the trade.
2. Place your stop loss on just outside the channel or just above the high of the candlestick (for a sell order) or just below the low of the candlestick (for
a buy order) that touched the channel and shows signs of rejection.
This candlestick can also be a reversal candlestick.
3. You may also decide to take half the profits off as price is in the middle of the channel for a profitable trade.

CHAPTER 8:
SEVEN (7) PROFITABLE CHART PATTERNS EVERY TRADER NEEDS TO KNOW

There's a difference between chart patterns and candlestick patterns. Chart patterns are not candlestick patterns and candlestick patterns are not chart patterns:

- Chart patterns are geometric shapes found in the price data that can help a trader understand the price action, as well make predictions about where
the price is likely to go.
- Candlestick patterns on the other hand can involve only one single candlestick or a group of candlestick which have formed one-after-the other in regard to how they form in relation to one another in terms of their body length, opening and closing prices, wicks(or shadows) etc.

Not knowing what chart patterns are forming can be a costly mistake. If you are like that, this is your opportunity to get back on track.

Why costly mistake? Because you are completely unaware of what is forming on the charts and you end up taking a trade that is not in line with what the chart pattern is signaling or telling you!

These are the 7 chart patterns you will learn about today:
1. Triangle chart patterns-symmetrical, ascending and descending (3 patterns)
2. Head and shoulders and Inverse Head and Shoulders (2 patterns)
3. Double Bottom and Double Top (2 patterns)

But first up, I am going to talk about triangle chart patterns.

1. Symmetrical Triangle

There are 3 types of triangle chart patterns and the chart below shows the differences between each very clearly:

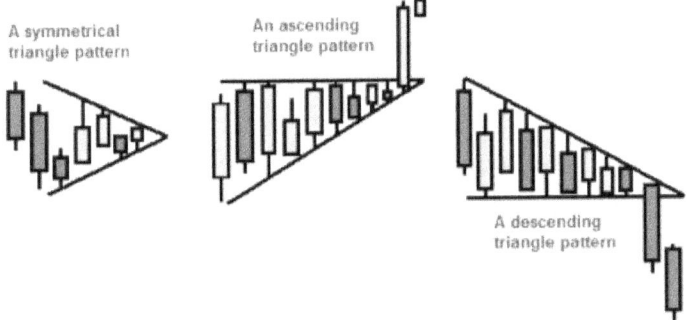

Now, lets starts with the symmetrical triangle pattern first.
Is A Symmetrical Triangle Bullish Or Bearish Chart Pattern?
The Symmetrical triangle chart pattern is a continuation pattern therefore it can
be both a bullish or bearish pattern.

What does this mean then? Well, if you see this pattern in an uptrend, expect a
breakout to the upside.

See an example below:

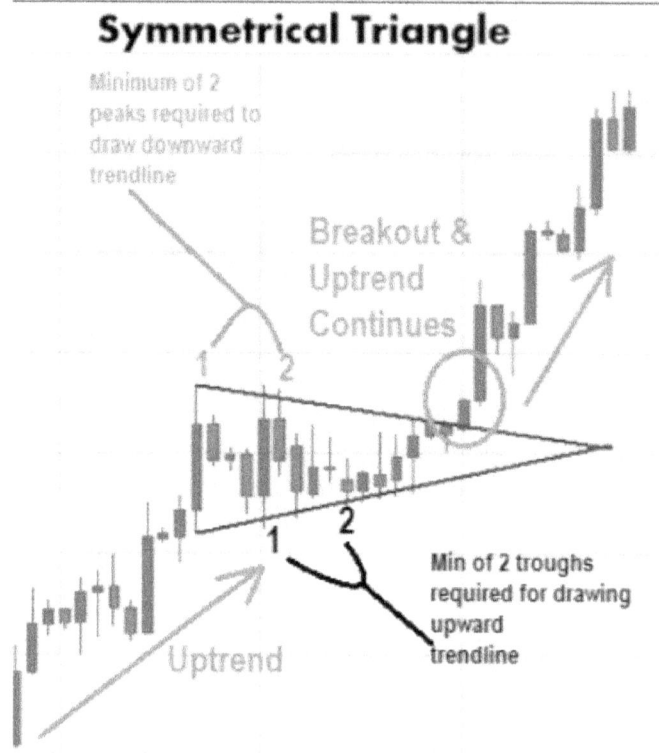

If you see a symmetrical triangle pattern form in a downtrend, then expect a
breakout of this pattern to the downside like this one shown below :

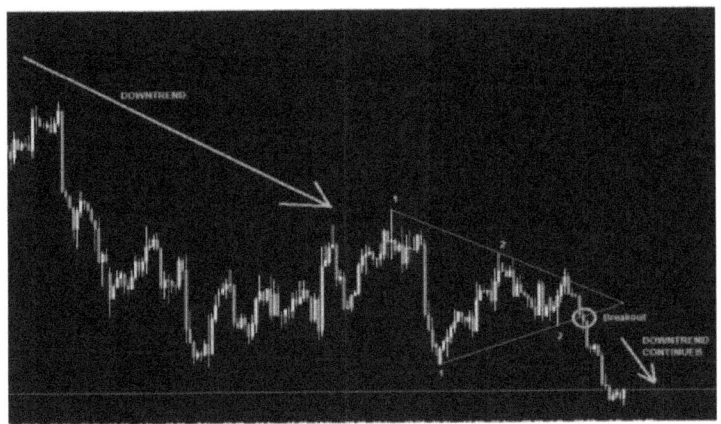

How To Draw A Symmetrical Triangle

• You will see price moving up and down but this up and down movement is converging to a single point.

• You need a minimum of 2 peaks and 2 troughs to draw the two trendlines on both sides.

• It will be only a matter of time before price breaks out of the pattern and either moves up or down.

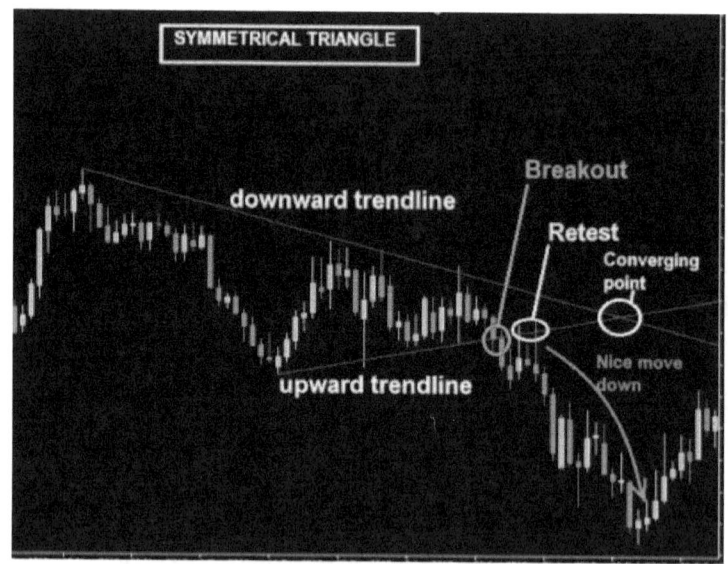

Two Simple Ways To Trade The Symmetrical Triangle

1. Trade the Initial Breakout

The best way is to confirm that the breakout actually happens with a candlestick before placing your order.

What I do I is for example, say I'm watching a

symmetrical triangle form in the 4hr charts and I know that soon a breakout will happen. I then switch to the 1hr chart to wait for the breakout to happen. If a 1hr candlestick has broken the triangle and closed below/above it, that's my trade entry signal. So I will place a pending buy stop/sell stop order to catch the breakout from there.

Often I want to make sure that the 1hr candlestick closes outside of the triangle
before I enter a pending buy stop or sell stop order to capture the move that
happens to avoid false breakouts while the candlestick has not closed yet.
But here's the problem with trading triangle breakouts, see chart below:

I don't like trading breakouts like the one shown above and here's why:
- The stop loss distance is too large. I'd prefer to enter trades with breakout candlesticks that are close to the trend lines that have been broken.
- I often see that such breakout of extremely long candlesticks are not sustainable and price will often tend to reverse after such candlesticks as can be seen by the chart above…notice that after the breakout candlestick, there was one bearish green pin bar and then for the next 4 candlesticks afterward, the price went down. This is what tends to happened with such long breakout candlesticks. So if you entered a buy order using that long breakout candlestick above, you would have to wait a while for your trade to turn profitable.

2. : Trade the retest of the trendline that is broken
- The second way to enter is to wait for a retest of the broken trendline in the triangle pattern then either buy or sell.
- This may also be handy if you had an extremely long breakout candlestick on the initial breakout, you best option is to wait for a retest of the breakout trendline then if that happens you enter. Stop loss Placement Options. Here are 3 ways on how to place stop loss on triangle patterns, which include symmetrical, ascending and descending triangle patterns which you will learn next. The stop loss placement techniques here are applicable to all triangle patterns so take note of that.

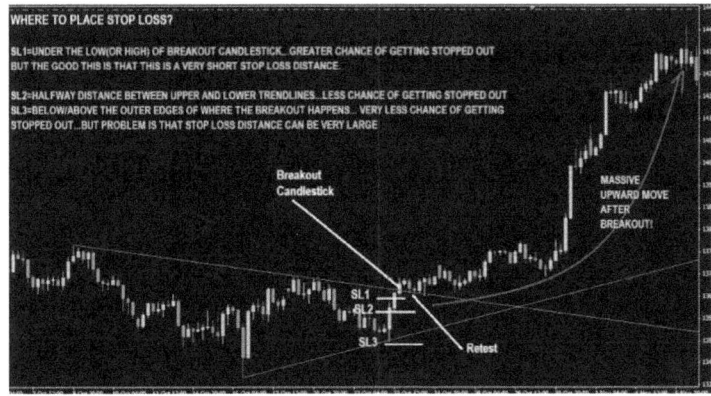

2. Ascending Triangle Chart Pattern

And ascending triangle pattern looks like this chart shown below:

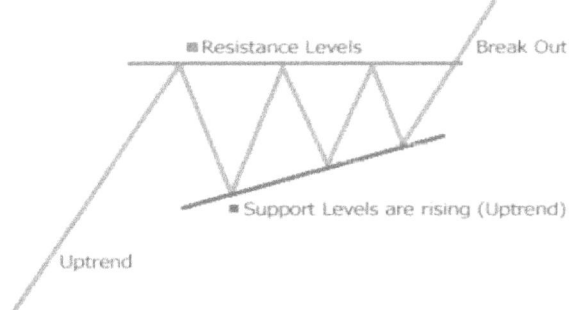

And this is how a real chart looks like:

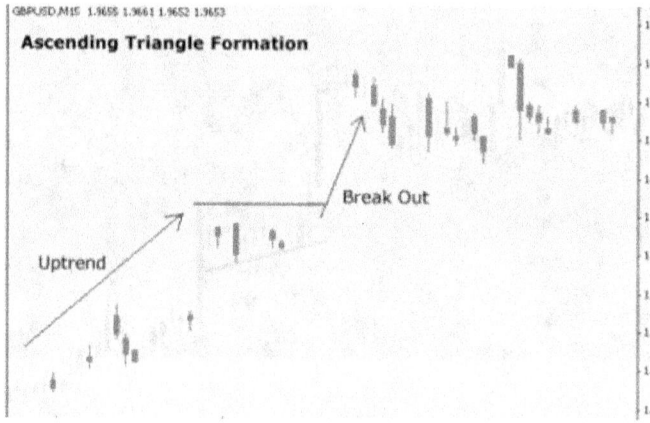

Is Ascending Triangle Pattern Bullish Or Bearish?
It is considered a bullish continuation pattern in an existing uptrend. So when you
see this forming in an uptrend, expect a breakout to the upside.
However, it can also be a strong reversal signal (bullish) when you see it form in a downtrend.

Stop Loss Placement Options
You can use the strategies given in symmetrical triangle.
Take Profit Options
I prefer to target previous resistance levels as my take profit target.
Or as shown on the chart below, you can use the "x" pips distance as your take
profit target. Another way to do it would be say 3 times the "x" pips or 2 times
the "x pips" distance. That should give you your profit target level(s).

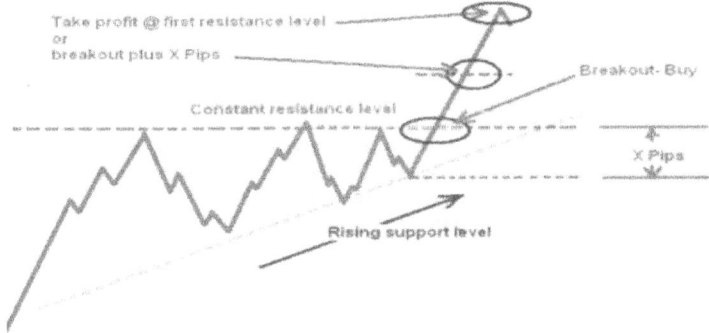

3. Descending Triangle Chart Pattern

Important things to note about the descending triangle chart pattern:

The descending triangle chart pattern is characterised by a descending resistance
levels and a fairly horizontal support levels converging to a point until a breakout
happens to the downside as shown below:

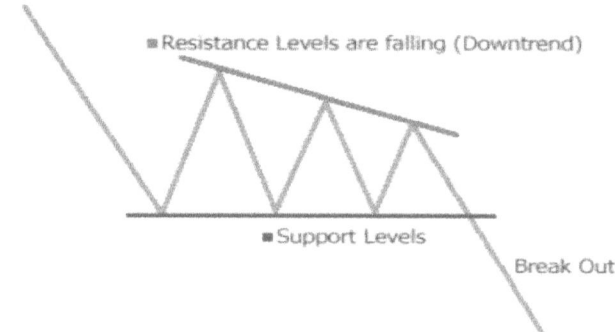

Descending Triangle Formation

Is Descending Triangle Pattern Bullish Or Bearish?

It is a bearish chart pattern that forms in a downtrend as a continuation pattern.

However, this pattern can also form as a bearish reversal pattern at the end of an uptrend.

Therefore regardless of where it forms, it's a bearish chart pattern.

How to Trade The Descending Triangle Formation

Similar to the other 2 triangle patterns, you can either trade the initial breakout or wait to see if price reverses back to test the broken support level and then sell.

Note: with a triangular pattern, I often prefer to wait for a candlestick to breakout
and close outside of the pattern before I enter a trade. This helps to reduce false breakout signals.
But there will be times when I will just trade the breakout with a pending sell stop order just a few pips under the support level to catch the breakout when it
happens but when I do that, I sit and watch the close of the 1hr candlestick to
make sure that it does not close above the support line (if that happens, it may mean a false breakout).
And then there's the issues of extremely long breakout candlesticks which are false breakouts and should be avoided.

As mentioned previously:

- when you have such extremely long breakout candlesticks like that, better to sit and wait to see if price will reverse and get back up to the support level that was broken (a retest) which will now be acting as a resistance level and then sell when that level is touched.

How To Take Profit

I prefer to use previous support levels, lows or troughs and use those as my take profit target level.
Another method of take profit that is commonly used is to measure the height of
the triangle and if the height is say 100 pips then that is your take profit target.
The chart below should give you a clear idea of how it's done:

Note that on the chart, the descending triangle formed the end of an uptrend.

4. Head & Shoulders Chart Pattern

The head and shoulder chart pattern is a bearish chart pattern. This is what a head and shoulder reversal pattern looks like:

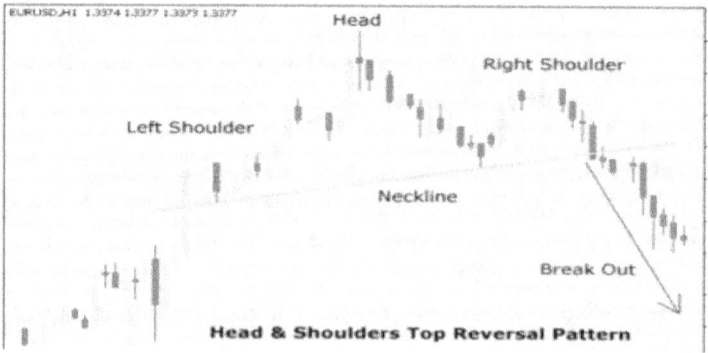

Important things to note about the head and shoulder pattern:

• The head and shoulders pattern is a bearish reversal pattern and when found in an uptrend, it signals the end of the uptrend.

Here's how this pattern forms:

- Eventually, the market begins to slow down after going up for some time and the forces of supply and demand are generally considered in balance.
- Sellers come in at the highs (left shoulder) and the downside is probed (beginning neckline.)
- Buyers soon return to the market and ultimately push through to new highs (head.)
- However, the new highs are quickly turned back and the downside is tested again (continuing neckline.)
- Tentative buying re-emerges and the market rallies once more, but fails to take out the previous high. (This last top is considered the right shoulder.) Buying dries up and the market tests the downside yet again. Your trendline for this pattern should be drawn from the beginning neckline to the continuing neckline.

Here's another example:

How To Trade The Head & Shoulder Chart Pattern.

The following chart below makes it much clearer.

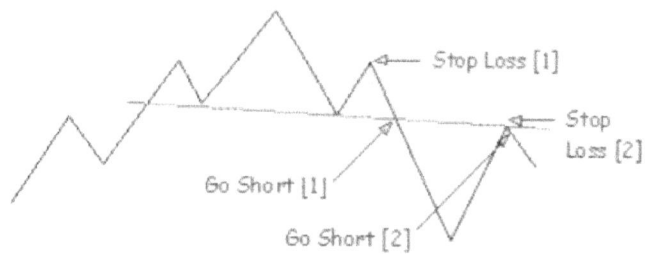

[1] Go short when price breaks below the neckline. Place a stop loss above the last peak. [2] If price rallies back to the neckline, go short on a reversal signal and place a stop loss above the resistance level.

How To Calculate Profit Targets
- I use previous lows or troughs to set my take profit target.
- However, you can also use the distance in pips between the neckline and the head as your take profit target level.

So if the distance is 100 pips, then
if you trade the initial breakout, you set it at 100pips take profit target level
like the chart shown below with the two blue lines:

5. Inverse Head and Shoulder Pattern

You will also see this pattern, though not as popular, it's good to keep an eye out for it. The inverse head and shoulder pattern is bullish reversal candlestick pattern
and just the opposite of head and shoulders pattern.
Here's what it look like on the chart shown below:

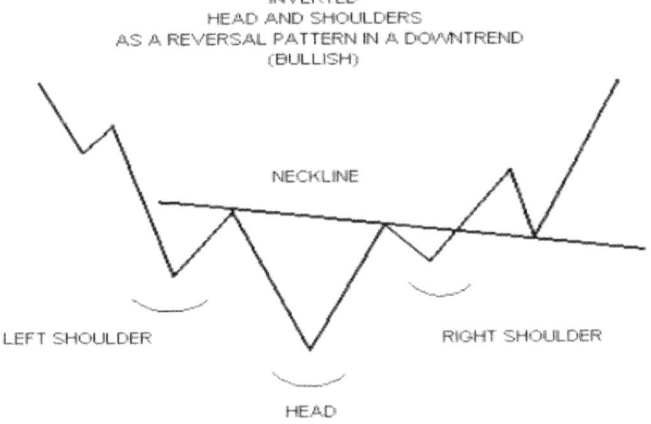

How to Trade the Inverse Head and Shoulder Pattern
You can buy the initial breakout of the neckline or wait for the re-test, that is wait for price to breakout and then come back down to test the broken neckline and
then buy. Use bullish reversal candlesticks for trade entry confirmation if you are waiting to buy on re-test.

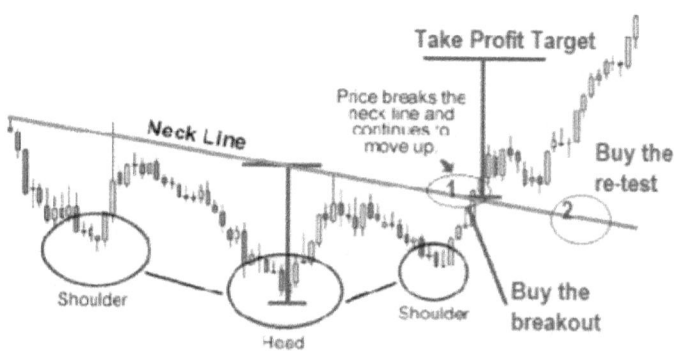

I often tend to place my profit target on previous highs. One method of calculating profit target is to measure from the head up to the trendline and what the distance in pips is your profit target. See the two blue vertical lines in the chart above.

6. Double Bottom Chart Pattern
A double bottom chart pattern is bullish reversal chart pattern and when it forms in an existing downtrend, it signals a possible upward trend.

Here's what It look like:

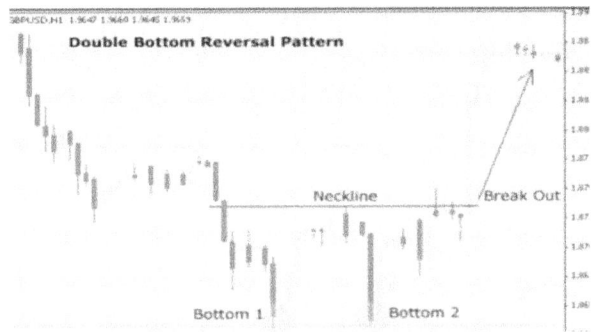

3 Ways on How To Trade Double Bottoms
1) Trade the breakout of the neckline:
Many traders once they see that the double pattern has formed and the neckline is being tested, that's when they get in as soon as a breakout happens.

2) Wait to enter on retest of Broken Neckline
Then there are other groups of traders that like to enter when price reverses back down to touch the neckline, which now would act as a support level. Once it hits that neckline level they buy.

3) Buy on bottom 2.
In this way, you have the potential to ride the trade all the way up if the neckline is intercepted. You should consider buying on bottom 2 as buying on a support level...as a matter of fact, that it what is is! Look for bullish reversal candlestick patterns for trade entry signals.

For Take Profit Target levels:
- If you buy on bottom 2, you can use the neckline as your take profit level, or any previous highs above that as well.

- If you buy the breakout of the neckline, use the distance between the bottom and the neckline in pips to calculate your profit target.

See chart below for example below:,

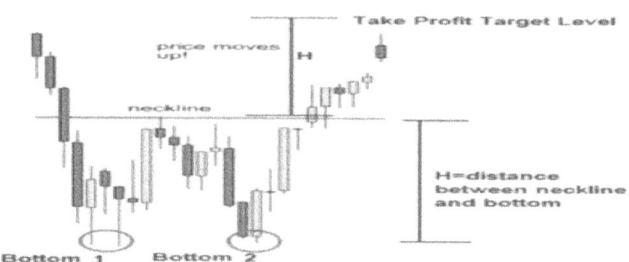

7. Double Top Chart Pattern

A double top chart pattern is a bearish reversal chart pattern and when found in an uptrend and once the neckline is broken, that confirms a downtrend.

The double tops are very powerful patterns and if you get into a trade at the right time, you stand to make a lot of profits when the breakout happens to the downside.

Its simply the opposite of Double bottom pattern .

How to Trade the Double Top Chart Pattern

There's 3 ways to trade the double top chart pattern:

#1: Trade the initial breakout of the neckline.

#2: The technique I like most to take a sell trade on Peak 2 when I see a bearish

reversal candlestick. And if price moves down and intersects the neckline and continues to do down further, your profits are dramatically increased.

Double Top Chart Pattern

(Diagram showing First Peak and Second Peak with Neckline, Existing Uptrend, Aggresive Entry Point, and Conservative Entry Point)

#3: You can wait for price to go back up to test the broken neckline (which would
now act as resistance level) and when you see a bearish reversal candlestick
pattern, go short (sell) as this example below shows:

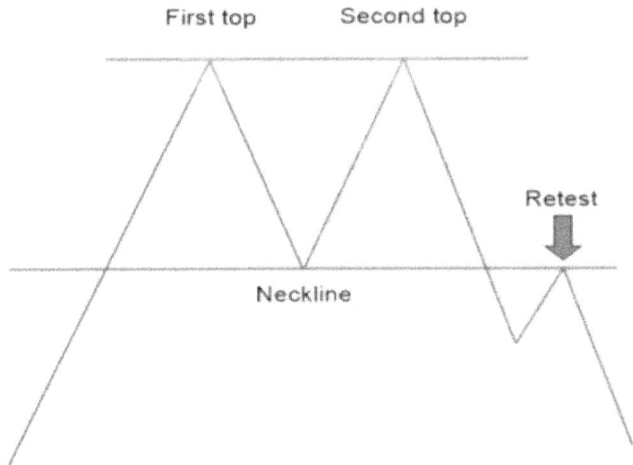

This image below is what it will look like in a live forex chart:

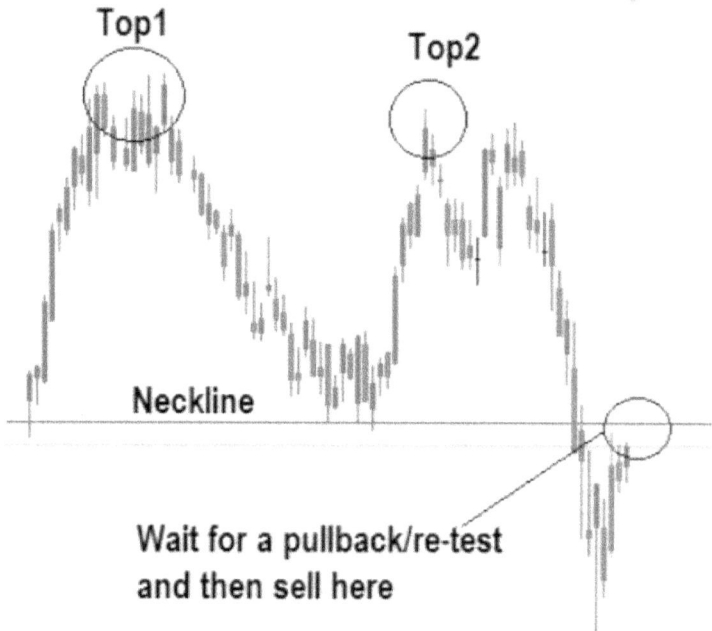

How to Take Profit On The Double Top Chart Pattern.
Use previous low (support levels) to set take profit targets.
Or another option would be to measure the distance between the neckline and the highest peak
(the range) and use that difference in pips as take profit target if you are trading the breakout from the neckline.

These chart patterns are the main part of this simplified strategy, study and practice it well with trendline, support & resistance knowledge discussed in this book. This will change you to a profitable master trader.

CHAPTER 9:
SIX (6) PROFITABLE CANDLESTICK PATTERNS EVERY TRADER NEEDS TO KNOW

There are lots of candlesticks, but out of all of them only 6 that you really need to know.

Why? Because there are very popular are really powerful so why waste time with the rest? When these candlesticks form at support and resistance levels or Fibonacci levels they are great trade entry signals.

#1: The Doji Candlestick Patterns.

The doji candlesticks are single (individual) candlestick patterns. There are 4 types
of doji candlesticks as shown below:

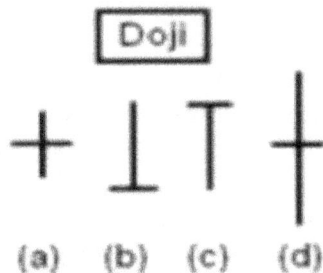

(a) Doji
(b) Gravestone Doji
(c) Dragonfly Doji
(d) Long-legged Doji

a) The doji cross can be both considered a bullish or bearish signal depending on where it forms.
b) The gravestone doji is considered a bearish reversal candlestick when formed in an uptrend or in a resistance level.
c) The dragonfly doji is considered a bullish candlestick pattern when formed in a downtrend or in a support level.
d) The long-legged doji shows a period of indecision by bulls and bears and depending on where it forms (uptrend/resistance level=bearish signal, downtrend/support level=bullish signal) it can be considered a bearish or bullish signal.

#2: The Engulfing Candlestick Patterns

The engulfing patterns are 2 candlestick patterns. For a bullish engulfing pattern,
you will see that the first candle is bearish followed by the second candle which is very bullish and this 2nd candle completely engulfs

a) Bullish Engulfing-when formed in a support level or in a downtrend, this can signal that the downtrend is potentially ending.

b) Bearish Engulfing-when formed in an uptrend or or in a resistance level, this is a signal that the uptrend may be ending.

#3: Shooting Star Candlestick Pattern

This is one of the most reliable candlesticks and obviously one of the most popular due to the fact that they are so easy to spot on any chart.
The shooting star is single candlestick pattern and when it forms in an uptrend or in a resistance level, then it is

considered as a bearish reversal pattern and so you should be looking to sell.

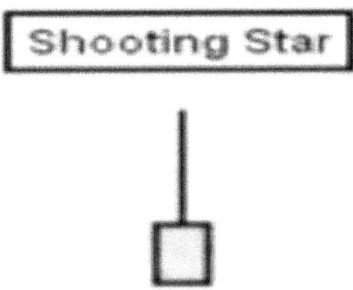

Note: the shooting star is sometimes called the bearish hammer, inverse hammer, inverted hammer or bearish pin bar. They all mean the same and refer to the shooting star candlestick pattern.

#4: Hammer Candlestick Pattern
The hammer candlestick is a single candlestick pattern pattern and its is considered a bullish reversal candlestick pattern and it's the opposite of the shooting star candlestick pattern.

It has a very long tail and a short upper wick or none at all. When it forms in a downtrend or at support levels, you should take note...this is a very high probability bullish reversal candlestick pattern and you should be looking to go long(buy).

#5: Hanging Man Candlestick Pattern
Now, what happens if you see in an uptrend a candlestick that looks like a hammer? Is it still a bullish signal? Well, in that case, this candlestick is a hanging
man and its not a bullish signal.

Here's how it looks:

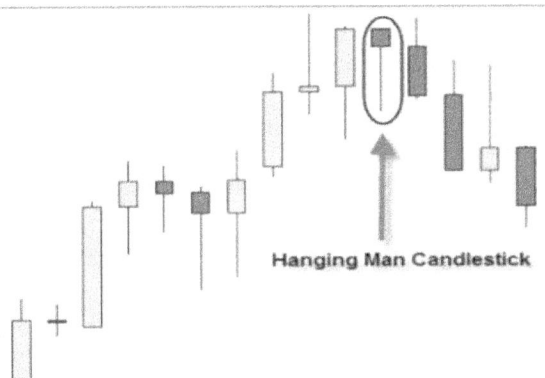

Now, the hanging man, is exactly like hammer but the only difference is that it must form in an uptrend.
When it forms in an uptrend or in resistance levels, it tells you that there is a possibility that the uptrend is ending so you should be looking to go short (sell).

#6: Spinning Top
Spinning tops can be continuation candlestick patterns or reversal candlestick patterns.

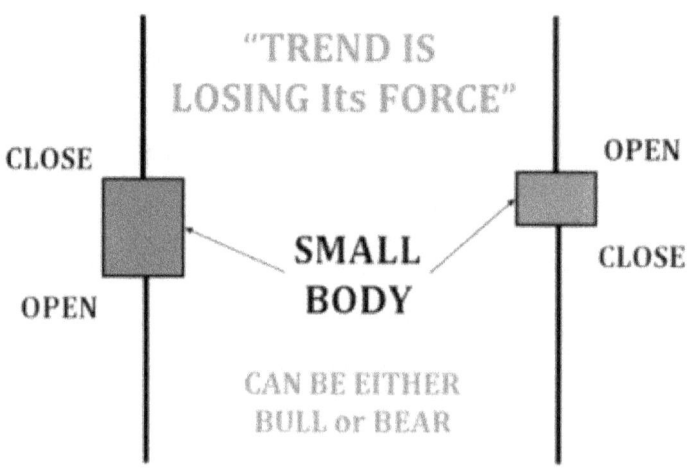

Spinning tops have small
bodies with upper and lower shadows
that exceed the length of the body.
Spinning tops signal indecision.
A spinning top is a single candlestick
pattern and it can be both bullish or bearish.
Let me explain.
 If you see are bearish
spinning top in a support area or in a
downtrend, this can be considered a bullish reversal signal
when the high of the bearish spinning top is broken to the
upside.
Similarly, a bullish spinning stop in a resistance level or in an
uptrend can be
considered a bearish signal as soon as the low is broken to
the downside.

Example below shows what I mean:

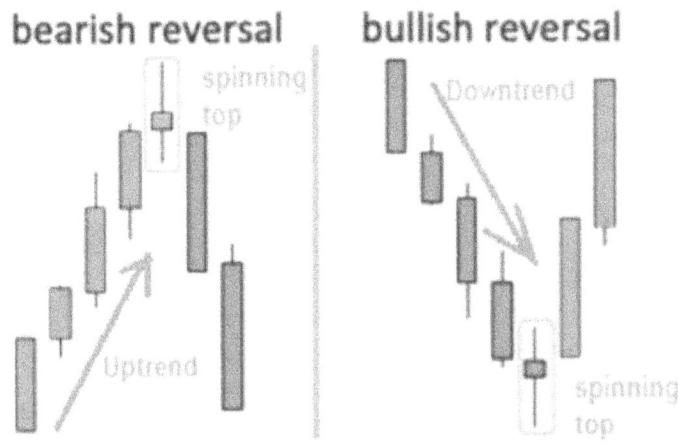

Spinning tops are fairly short in length compared to other candlesticks and their body length is a few steps wider than that of doji candlesticks(which actually have
none or very tiny bodies).
Another notebale feauture of spinning tops is that the wicks on both sides should be almost the same length.
When I see spinning tops form on support or resitance levels, all it tells me the bears and bulls do not really know where to push the market and so when a breakout of the low or high of a spinning top by the next candle that forms usually signals the move in that direction of breakout!

CHAPTER 10:
HOW TO TRADE TRENDLINES WITH PRICE ACTION

When the market is heading down, it forms down swings and up swings as it continually moves lower.

Similarly, when the market is in an uptrend, it will form upswings and downswings as it continues to move up.

The peaks that are formed by the up swings and the troughs that are formed by the down swings can be used to draw trendlines.

- And you need a minimum of 2 peaks to draw a downward trendline for a market that is in a downtrend
- and you need 2 troughs to draw an upward trendline for a market that is in an uptrend.

Downtrend Trendlines

Now, for a market in a downtrend, you can connect the peaks with a line and that forms you downward trendline. What you are waiting for is for price to come back up and touch that trendline and when it does,

this could mean that a down swing will start and it may be the best time to enter a short trade.

The use of bearish reversal candlesticks as trade confirmation is highly recommended with this trading method.

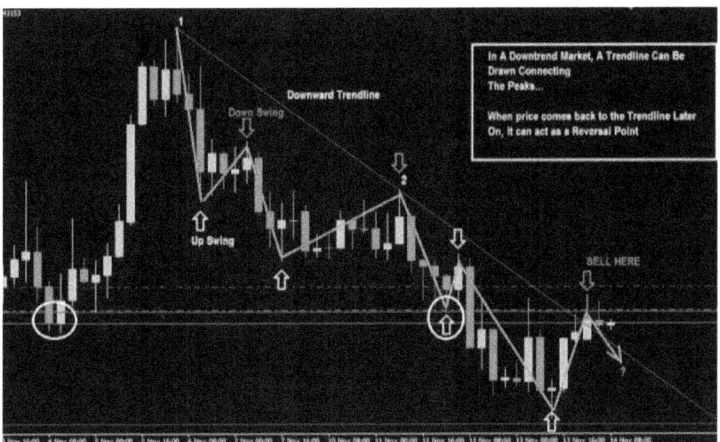

Upward Trendlines
When the the market is in an uptrend, connect 2 troughs and you have an upward trendline. When price comes to touch it later, you have a potential buy setup.

What happens if the trendline gets intersected?
There are a couple of things you need to be aware when a trendline gets intersected:
(1)The first is that it could mean the trend has now changed.
(2)The second is that it can be a false break only and price will soon head back in the original direction.

Now, there's another thing about trendlines, if one trendline get's broken, you need to be see if you can draw another trendline above (or below) the one that's
broken.
 There can be 2 or more downward trendlines or 2 or more upward

trendlines at any one time on any chart in any timeframe.
So if price breaks the first trendline, it still has yet to head to the 2nd and the third
etc...
So if you take a sell trade on the first trendline but price intersects it and you are stopped out with a loss and now price is heading to the 2nd trendline above, you
should also look to sell if you get bearish reversal candlestick signal.

CHAPTER 11:.
MULTI-TIMEFRAME ANALYSIS

Multi timeframe trading is the act of analyzing a currency pair on a higher timeframe(4Hr and above) and then execute the trade on a lower timeframe.

For example, I personally analyzes market on a daily timeframe and then executes it on a 4Hr time, my take profits and stoplosss levels is also based on the lower timeframe (4Hr),

The purpose of multi timeframe analyses is to get STRONGER analysis and trade entries which gives you more confidence on your trades,
Trades on lower timeframe hardly obeys analysis directions but a trade analyzed on a high timeframe (4h and above) gives more stronger signal and so has more win potential (this gives you more confidence on your trades).

ADVANTAGES OF MULTI TIMEFRAMING
- It helps you get more pips target you can get as big as 200 – 1000 pips on a single trade ,which won't have been possible on a lower timeframes
- Gives stronger signals.
- Gives you relief from looking at your chart always, you can go do your normal works while your trades are running.

CHAPTER 12:.
TRADE THE OBVIOUS

I hope you have learnt how powerful price action trading can be. Now, not all trading setups you see will become winners. But here's the thing…if your losses are small but your profits are large, you will always be in be out in front. That's why trading risk management is important.

When you are watching the chart for trading setups, you need see and trade the obvious.
What do I mean by that?
Well, if there is an obvious pattern on the chart and you can see it clearly, then
you should know that there are thousands of traders out there are watching the
exact same thing as you are doing…because it's so obvious.
Things like:
- Trendlines or channels or bullish pin bar forming on major support level, if you can see that, there are many that will be seeing the same thing.
- All these traders will be waiting to see what happens at these levels and say if a bullish hammer forms on a major support level, then guess what will happen next? The most likely outcome of that is that as soon as the high of the hammer candlestick is broken, price will shoot up!

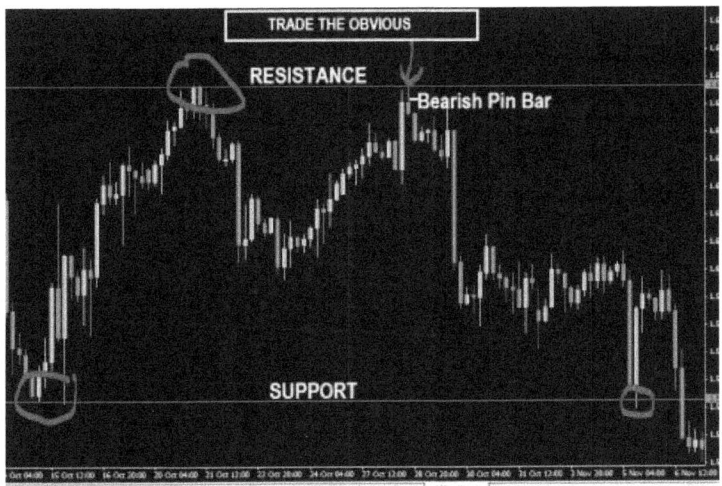

How many times have you ever went over your chart and you are like:

"Goodness me! I should have taken a trade here and look at how the market moved after that bearish shooting star candlestick was formed after hitting the resistance level."

When you trade the obvious, then you trade with what everybody else is seeing and in essence you are really doing piggy-back, riding on the market move created by all these orders that puts the odds in your favour.

See chart below for this: if you see a support major support level and price is heading down to it and at the same time, that support level is coinciding with an upward trendline...

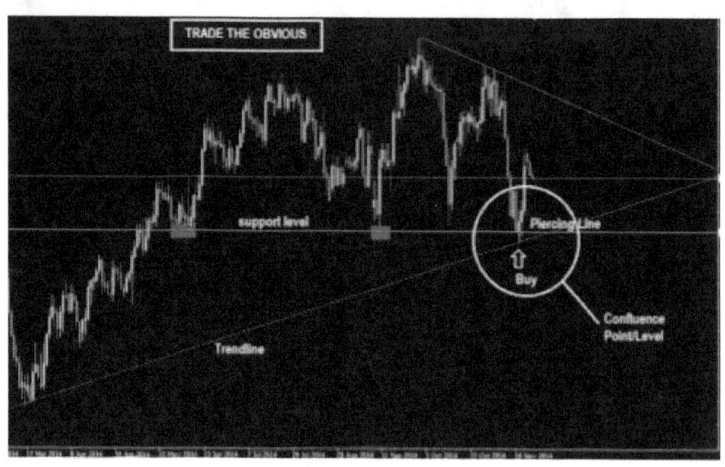

CHAPTER 13:.

SECRET MARKET TIPS

Things to expect on trading days:.

- On Mondays ,currency pairs oscillate(No direction), it is not advisable to trade today.
- On Tuesday ,reversals and retracements occur, their can also be a continuation of Monday oscillations.
- On Wednesday ,market chooses and moves in a direction(long or short direction) during the London & new York overlap time upwards. You can enter you trades today(safe).
- On Thursday , Wednesday moves continues especially during the London & network session overlaps, you can also enter trades today.
- On Friday, market direction tends to change as many traders are closing their trades today for the weekend, it is not advisable to trade today.

(Note: Not applicable to Gold(XAUUSD))

Note:. This doesn't mean this things will happen literally all the time on all pairs, there can be slight change.

GOLD (XAUUSD) MARKET TIPS

(Things to expect on trading days for Gold)

- On Mondays, if the market is currently Trending from previous week, then market will move against the trade on Monday after the closure of the first two 4H

candles(entries can be made at this time according to your analysis. (100pips move expected) . Big candle moves can occur today.
- On Tuesdays, Monday direction continues if there was no big candle move on Monday, but if there was a big Monday move, then expect a retracement .
- Full retracement day, the market fully retraces today(ie the opposite of Tuesday direction happens today) .
- On Thursday, (safe Entry day), Today moves in the opposite of Wednesday direction, and continues for the day (at least 200pips target).
- On Fridays, The Thursday direction continues today till market closes .

Note:. All entries should not just be based on this theories but on your Chart analysis, these theories are just to help you confirm strongly when to enter a Trade.

CHAPTER 14:
CLOSING REMARKS

Some things you should learn:

- Levels are not lines drawn in concrete, they get broken. You see, the more a level is tested multiple times, sooner or later it will get broken. From my observations, 2-3 times is the average, after that, expect a breakout of the level.

- Don't listen to analysts. They can stuff up your decision making process and cloud your judgement. For example: I see a sell setup on my chart but because I've read the analysts report that says he is bullish on this currency pair because of this and that reason, I hesitate to pull the trigger . Later, I check the chart and see that If I had sold, I would have made money. So use your own independent judgment based on what you see on your charts.

- Find your best timeframe to trade. Your personality, work circumstances etc may dictate what timeframe you can use. For me, I can trade from the daily,4hr and 1hr charts because I use multi-timeframe trading. But if it's the lower timeframe like 5min,15min and 30min that suits you and you like it, then No problem, just make sure you're comfortable with it.

- If the bus leaves you, don't chase the bus! In other words... don't chase trades. If you are late to get into a trade at an optimal entry point and realized that you might "miss out", then back off and wait. There will always be another opportunity or wait for a retrace/retest/pullback etc and then enter.

- Be patient for the right trading setups to form.
- If you are suffering from losing streaks, take a break. Take a week off from trading to clear up your mind then come back with a clear mind to trade.
- If you have winning streaks, don't get overconfident and risk more. You streaks of losses may be just around the corner.

THE COMBINATION OF ALL THESE MAKES UP THE SIMPLIFIED POWERFUL FOREX STRATEGY , STUDY THEM CAREFULLY AND PRACTICE ON DEMO FIRST.

Happy Trading!

@Isaackings

www.ingramcontent.com/pod-product-compliance
Lightning Source LLC
Chambersburg PA
CBHW070851220526
45466CB00005B/1955